# Breakfast With You

## A Collection of Poetry

Mark C. LLoyd

NFB

<<<>>>

Buffalo, NY

ISBN: 978-0692491058

Breakfast With You/ LLoyd-1ˢᵗ ed.

1. Poems.  2. Verse.

3. LLoyd  4. No Frills Buffalo

No Frills Buffalo/Amelia Press

<<<>>>

119 Dorchester Road

Buffalo, New York 14213

For more information visit
Nofrillsbuffalo.com

Thank you to my parents, my family, my friends,
Tracy and Boo.

And to Nikki Germany and Rochelle Garrison

"Lean on the Window Ledge"

Lean on the window ledge
Blow out the smoke
Sip your coffee
Watch the sun rise on the suburban pavement
Feel 6am on your china doll face and tired eyes
Think of yesterday and last night
Lean on the window ledge and have that one
peaceful moment of the day
Sip 6am away

## THE POEMS:

## Breakfast with You

I wonder what it would have been like to have
Breakfast with you
Do you like eggs?
Sunny side up or scrambled?
Bacon?
Burnt?
Cripsy?
What do you like on your toast?
Could I serve you in bed?
Would you let me kiss you between bites?
Curl up next to you?
Keep you warm?
Watch a goddess eat
I wonder what it would have been like to have
Breakfast with you

... and this is for the "stunning" beauty who inspired me to
write many of these.

## Making Love Can Taste So Good

Oh, look at that beautiful face
Lips like red drapes on white shades
2am sleep between your breasts
Warmth of crossed thighs
Warm chocolate pudding for a 5am breakfast
Slow motion stretch
Toes dancing against my hips
Long sexy nails whisper to my earlobes
This thirst is encourageable
Is this what want?
Is it what you need?
My tongue dancing on your lips
Hair buried into feathers
Biting gasp
Wet on my lips
My deep swallow explodes
Take my hands into yours as I travel
Rock
Slide
Ride from side to side
Making love tastes so good

## Two Hugs

After two hugs I was there
taste of your earlobe
Nose buried in your hair
I can't squeeze
I'd never leave
I try not to breathe
Time must stop
It took two hugs
That's all it took
After two hugs
 I was
there

## Evening Streets Can Be So Lonely

Walking slowly through the city
The aroma of cheap hot dogs grilling on some vendor's
corner cart
Hear the occasional car horn honk and tire squeal
My eyes are tired
Heavy
My cigar smoke makes them dry
the click clack of a few heels as women pass
I sip my coffee and push my cigar
Again
Wondering where they are going
Have been?
Evening streets can be so lonely
giggling
Laughing
Arguing into cell phones
I can hear smiles
it begins to rain
Chug the coffee to get warm
Smoke to get a nicotine buzz
Toss the cigar into the wet street
Watch it rock a bit and roll into the drain
More heels
Chatter
I slowly scatter
Evening streets can be so lonely

## It

It's free
you never know when it'll hit
It could last forever
It could last a day
It can come with Pain
Heartbreak
Confusion
It's beautiful
It's frustrating
Is it worth it?
Yes
Even when it's not
And it's so powerful
Do I even have to say the word?
To some?
And to others
It's left our minds
Not on our lips
Still in our heart
Asleep

## It's The Beauty You Hide

It's the beauty you hide
don't need make-up that covers
hair you wear
yours isn't dark enough?
lipstick or is it gloss?
Doesn't matter
You don't need it
It's the beauty you hide

That smile that makes any man confide
He doesn't want to
He does
He has to
It's that raw smile on that beauty you hide
It's the perfect smile
Lips to be loved
Eyes to be stared into
It's the beauty you hide

## Morning Beauty

You're the body of aromatic beauty
I watch you bloom in the spring
Spreading love to my mid summers dream
Your morning smile a bouquet of floral
Lips a heart-shaped purse
Your neck and shoulders my breakfast of taste
We hug hip to waist
Clocks ticks for us to wake
I hope it rains
I hope it showers
I want just one more hour
Let me hold you just one more hour

## Icy Water

Even with the icy water surrounding my shoed feet all my
dreams can still bounce through my head as I watch the
dark, curvy silhouette gliding on top and under the evening's
glow of the water.
An ebony mermaid rolls and glides
around a large rock. Perches herself on top as if making love
to the sky.
Moon glow on her forehead
teeth bright as pearls.
She was too far for me to swim.
She was beyond my reach.
I could only whisper and cry.
My heart became heavy
cold
Just a few swishes toward her but she was gone ...
She was gone.

## No Problem

You said no lies
No fronting
No problem
Only you left
Disappeared
Ignored me
I need no explanation
Reason
Response
No problem
I'm sure
I wasn't the first

## Love Is Your Decision

And so we come to the moment when you say
you have no romance left
After the wine is kissed off your lips
I lick the tear streaming to your chin
Romance has died?
You are better off alone?
Are you?
You really are the only one who can judge
Love is your decision
Romance is out of your equation?
Variables are presented
Equality of
Love
The clock doesn't stop ticking when the heart does
Love is misplaced
We do a ballroom dance around it
Confuse it with the deserts of passion
and one day
standing in the rain
like a raindrop in October
it will tap
you
gently
and love is our decision

## Oh, How I

Oh how you shimmy and shake Guarding everything
Nothing for me to chase Oh how you sit there Soft as
lace Guarding everything for me not to take Oh how I
wish you'd look at me I wish you'd look my way Guarding
everything so I cant take your smile and add to it Smile and
bounce You bounce shimmy shake my mind
Oh how I want to see it
John Legend and Donna Summer
keep your attention Wish I could compete
You're quiet, mild and fantastic and wild.
Oh how I wish you'd look my way

## Lady, My

Lady behind the smile
eyes distant from trust
a stunning statuesque
walls too high to climb
forces me to create a door of words
Lady my words are old
but more than true
Have faith
breathe the same air
Drink the scent of your hair
Just watch you open that door
at some point
some day

## Beautiful to the Listen

Late night voice
Half asleep
Evening giggles
Moans
Beautiful to the listen
Pajamas from Macy's
Silky across the breast
Sheets made for fun
No orgasms discussed
Minds both full of lust
Under the blankets soft sounds
11pm moans
Sighs
I'm sure I heard those rubbing thighs
It's all beautiful to the listen

## Tears and Rejection

It's time and the tears
that tell the heart
to cry
Tears and rejection
Heartache is mine
Time has stopped
Heart has told me
It's time
Time will cry

## My Soul Business

Closed
Inaccessible
Not open
Out of business
Out of order
Reconstructing
Under new management
Limited hours
Limited menu
Most likely to close sooner than planned
Everything
Must go

## One Night

I was in Love
One time
One woman
I was in Love

She left
It was death
One morning
One day
She left
It was death

Closed my mind
I put up the walls
I shut the door
One day
Ten years
I closed my mind

One night
Saw a beauty
Saw her eyes
Saw her lips
Saw her beauty

She smiled softly
Kept my distance
I was amazed
I saw this beauty
I kept my distance
She smiled so softly

Her walls were up

Her door was closed

I unlocked my door
I looked at my wall
I dropped it quickly
I opened my door
One night
I dropped my wall

One night
She smiled softly
Kept my distance
I was amazed
I kept my distance

One night
She smiled so softly
I heard the door shut
Her walls went up
One night
I heard the door shut
Her walls went up
One night

One night
My walls went up
I shut my door
I lose the key
I look outside
No more smile so softly

The walls are up
I am amazed
The door is shut
The walls are up

One night
Tonight
I am amazed
I can't see her eyes
I can't see her smile
But I know
The world still has her beauty

## The Decision Has Been Made

Sometimes
the decision
Has been
made
for us
There isn't
The control we wish for
There is no destiny
Sometimes
No happy
Ever
after
We go on
Unsure
But the decision
Has been made
And all we can do
Is
Go
On
However
The decision
Has been made
There is no
Destiny

## This Is Love … That isn't

So what if you didn't get that
You still have this
Do you really need that?
And that?
That is something else you didn't get
But this is still right in front of you
never left
This has always been here
Sometimes we are so busy trying to get that
we forget how important this is
Why is that so important?
especially when we don't even know what that really is
Can that hug you at night?
Can that make you feel warm?
This can
This can make you get goose bumps where that could never
find
I thought I wanted that
Don't we all?
We all have those moments where our minds stray
That seems so thrilling
That is so different
This is the same old thing
Or is it?
Maybe this seems the same because it refuses to
compromise
Like that does
I need this
I finally know this
I need this
If I could only hold onto this for a little bit longer
Maybe I could appreciate this more?
That comes and goes

This!
Well, this is here for forever
This will be here when I need it!
And even when we don't want it
Never forget how important this is
Love isn't that
That isn't love
This is!
This is love!
And isn't this just great!

## Walls ... and a Rose

My walls were moved by your soul
Just
Enough
You didn't cross
No peak
No interest
Nothing you wanted to seek
What
So
Ever
Now I'll close them
Maybe for good
You can only feel what your heart
opens to
I will never ask
more
from you

I'll leave a Rose outside them
Just knock
Loud enough
for my heart to hear you

## A Stunning Woman in a Dirty Bar
### (Based on a true story)

Worn out chairs
Chipped tables
Cracks on floors
Doors that squeak
Hanging on
by one bolt
Dark
Dingy
Aroma of grease
And there she is
A stunning woman
In a dirty bar
Removes her scarf
The more I see
The more I like
Removes her coat
There she sits
Another look
I just shook
Damn
Damn
Damn
This stunning woman
Out of place
Out of sight
This stunning woman
just made this place
such a pretty bar
such a pretty place

## An Ugly Man in a Beautiful Room
### (Based on a true story)

Swaying hips
Water sips
Lunch time trip
"I look my worse" you say
but
"I find you damn beautiful today"
Cover your face
Napkin white
Skin like glossy night
across the table
old fright
Oak decor
Thousands of lights
Mirror mirror on every wall
This woman
Beautiful
Enters this room
Today
To meet an ugly man in a beautiful room

## The Sand and the Wine

Dinner
Lobster
The beach when the sun hides
Long kisses
On your back in the sand
Nothing beats evening's tastings
You absolutely intoxicate me
Your evening's perfume
Vanilla, Caramel and Chocolate
I breathe in the Beaujolais
Scent of red grapes
Savor them
Taste the aroma in the air
Seeing your half covered thighs
hidden under the bubble and the bath
flickering candles
too dark to read
light enough to sip
your smooth skin across my face
as I splash
you slide to your side
I can taste the sand off your back and wine on your lips
You absolutely intoxicate me
The sand and the Wine
It absolutely intoxicates me

## Her Legs Do Amazing Things

A splash of cream in her caramel
Legs that will speak
Make me to peak
Seek
Be a freak
A woman with class
Normally
very meek
Walks
Strolls
Struts
Bouncing her beautiful
Sass
Her legs do amazing things
Sensual
Alert

Day time tame?
Maybe
What a shame?
bedroom
Growl
Day time flirt?
That's her business
Isn't it?
Soft as cotton
Dark as chocolate
With the delicious center
Can't wait to dive
Dip
Lick
Sip
Sticks to our lips
Oh, those legs
Those legs do amazing things

## Songs of Love

What's Goin' On? Soooooo, I Heard It Through the
Grapevine that you found out I Want You and we both
know It Takes Two.
Mmmmmm yeahhhh Mery Mercy Me!! I need your
Sexual Healing so Let 's Get It On! Damn! How Sweet
It Is To Be Loved By You!
You're My Precious Love, baby ! You know, I Could Build
My Whole Life Around You. When you're not around
you give me the damn Inner City Blues which Make Me
Wanna Holler so don't be my Distant Lover.
When you're not around I'm Too Busy Thinking About
My Baby ... Ain't That Peculiar? That's The Way Love Is.
There Ain't Nothing Like The Real Thing.

## Full Moons, Sun Rises and Sunsets

Full moons, sun rises and sunsets
Full moon on the water
Sunrises on the shore
Sun sets under water
A fascinated
Ebony stunning
Mermaid
Swims
Dances
Lives
Loves
In a music of the sea
Full moons
Sun rises
Sunsets
Beautiful music of the sea
Dance
Beautiful mermaid
Dance and swim your way
Always feel safe and free

## It Could Be The Way

It could be the way
you look at me
never knowing what's on your mind
It could be the way
you walk
assurance you are all woman
all of the time
It could be the way
you speak
as soft as your skin is dark satin
It could be the way
you sit
legs crossed
It happened
You
are as
dangerous
as missing time
It could be the way
of most anything
that I hope
I have years
to discover
and hope to find

... on your kisses

Tasting
Jazmin on your hair
the softness of your chin
the sexiness of that aroma
perfume
on your tissue
Feel the warmth
of your hugs
See the wine on your lips
under the moonlight
you sip
I want to get drunk on your kisses

## The Few Who Tried

Emotionally
When I was supposed to be left I was usually off right or hiding
in my world
Never a normal night
a little off kilter days
Eccentric and moody bring gifts to
you
to ease any of your confusion pain
I stepped back
as you left
I always let you make that move
I must always keep your pride intact
And if anything was gained
Being Eccentric but not insane
Is that you will always remember
One guy
Who put you before ego
And never took
Never left you without self esteem

## Love Babble

Your beautiful face
Makes me happy
Your body drives me wild
Your eyes are artistic pools
Legs erotic life
Lips are roses under winter
Hips for me to soothe
Autumn comes
You are gone
Too late
Too quick
Too soon
I'm a superficial wreck
Age hasn't turned
me into
great wine
I'm bitter
forgotten with the dust
You're sleeping in my heart
You've kissed my empty soul

## Two Bottles of Wine

One new
Fresh
Full of all nature's flavor
Sealed to perfection
Waiting to be sipped
Devoured
Appreciated by class
The other
Dusty
Bitter
Opened
stale from time
Age has made it flat
Wet ring stains on a wooden
table tops
the aroma of yesterday's cigarettes
perspiration surrounds the room
Two bottles of wine
So different they grow

Two bottles of wine
One new
Fresh

## Even With the Cold Outside

Even with the cold outside
the snow
that tap tap tapping at my window
wind jiggles our frames
you still
keep
me
warm
with only a smile
bouncing eyes
dancing thoughts
your fingers tracing my lips
a smile that paints my heart

Even with the cold outside

## Author Mark C. LLoyd

Mark C. LLoyd is a published Poet and a produced Playwright who resides in Lockport, New York.

As a Playwright, Director, board member and production consultant he has worked with many theater companies in the Buffalo, New York area.

To date he has directed over two dozen of his own one-act plays.

In 2009 Mark won an award for Directing from the Theatre Association of New York State and in May of 2006 he won the award for Writing "Hollywood Dreams-A Monologue".

He has been the featured reader and host at numerous Poetry events and has self-produced several artistic and theater productions.

His self-published Poetry chap book from 2010 "Warm Blooded Mornings" is still available for sale as well as his 2012 miniature book "It's The Place You'll Find Me" by Destitute Press.

In 2013 his book "Unfinished Suite: Poetry & Prose" was released by No Frills Publishing and is described as "… Lloyd has mastered the art of living in each moment. He captures and brilliantly documents the details of those moments that most take for granted, as if he sees the future and recognizes the fortune in front of him. He breathes life into every day human interactions."

Presently Mark is working on editing a novella and two books of his plays.

## The Blueness of My Brain and the Bitterness of My Soul

Weightless safe I arrive for all of them to see that I love her
and that I love her.
The blueness of my brain and the bitterness of my soul and I
can't change who I am and what I want.
I know what's out there and I know what is out there isn't safe.
It's what I need.
And safety is overrated when it comes to the heart.
The blueness of my brain and the bitterness of my soul.
There is no safety in love.
Even in the blueness of my brain and in the bitterness of my
soul.

www.ingramcontent.com/pod-product-compliance
Lightning Source LLC
Chambersburg PA
CBHW071026040426
42443CB00007B/950